Below are a few kind words from our friends:

Dear San Dan Yi,
My healing sessions with you over the past 2 years have had a profound effect on me. I am no longer looking outward for my happiness. You are right; happiness really is INSIDE of me. Thank you for your presence in my life.

Sincerely,
Babak Razi
Beverly Hills, CA.

I have been working with San Dan Yi for the past year. I have experienced powerful and positive changes in my life in the area of my career, health and overall personal development. I even got married to the love of my life.

San is an intelligent, insightful coach/mentor with a very sharp sense of humor. Working with him is effective and you have fun along the way. I am grateful for his presence in my life.

Kindest regards,
Suzanne M. Attorney at Law.

I am so grateful to you, San Dan Yi, for your multiple gifts of intuition, energy healing and more. You have nurtured my spirit, mind and body to the point of helping me balance the very nature of what I now recognize as my universal purpose and natural flow my life now leads. Thank you for your guidance, gifts and you.

Sincerely,
Carol Hovsepian
La Moog Productions, Inc.
Hollywood, CAI

Can't tell you what a blessing it is to have you in my life. The exact philosophy you talk about re: the lessons of the soul for this particular incarnation are exactly what I'm feeling in my life now and seem right to believe in at my core. I'm so grateful that you told me to read "Seat of the Soul" and "The Path to Love". Both books changed my life and inspired so much amazing spiritual work.

Thank you from the bottom of my heart.

Donna Grissom
Los Angeles, CA

Dear San Dan Yi,
Being the owner of the Center for the New Age in Sedona, Arizona, I have had the opportunity to work with many gifted Psychics and Healers. You are definitely a Psychic's Psychic and a Healer's Healer. I am grateful you are a part of my life.

Anita Dalton
Owner, Center for the New Age
Sedona, Arizona

∞

Also By San Dan Yi

The Spirit Of Sedona:

13 Month Engagement Planner and Journal

∞

The Book of Yi-isms

Notice of Rights

The Organic View Press titles may be purchased for business or promotional use or for special sales. For more information, please write to: Special Markets Department, The Organic View Press, 3300 Park Avenue, PO Box 4018, Wantagh, NY 11793

Notice of Liability

The author has made every effort to check and ensure the accuracy of the information presented in this book. However, the information herein is sold without warranty, either expressed or implied. Neither the author, publisher, nor any dealer or distributor of this book will be held liable for any damages caused indirectly or directly by the information contained in this book.

Disclaimer

The author and publisher are not engaged in rendering medical or psychological services. The author and publisher provide no guarantees, implied warranties, or assurances of any kind and will be held harmless for any interpretation made by the reader choosing to independently take advantage of information presented in this book. The information provided in this book is presented for entertainment purposes only and is not intended to diagnose, treat, or cure any disease or to substitute the advice provided by your own physician and/or other medical or mental health professional.

Every effort has been made to provide the most up to date and accurate information possible. Technological changes may occur at any time after the publication of this book. This book may contain typographical and content errors; therefore this is only designed as a guide and a resource.

ISBN-13: 978-0615964577 (The Organic View)

ISBN-10: 0615964575

The Book of Yi-isms

A journey towards self-discovery.

By San Dan Yi

Edited by June Stoyer

• *New York* •

Dedicated to Babak Razi for always making sure my runway was clear.

TABLE OF CONTENTS

INTRODUCTION TO THE YI-ISMS JOURNAL OF SELF-DISCOVERY

Why I created my "Yi-isms" and how to use them.

After working with over ten thousand clients in my mentoring and healing practice, over the past two decades, I realize that we are all bound to be here. We all come here to work on different issues. Each person is equipped with a unique set of skills that addresses issues which include the things that bring us joy and sorrow. These issues lead us towards self-realization and self-growth. Most of my clients truly have a strong desire to make change. However, change is not brought about easily because we are creatures of habit.

With this in mind, I began to compile a list of mini life-lessons or what I refer to as "Yi-isms." These lessons are designed to invoke self-contemplation that leads to self-awareness through a personal internal process that only we, as individuals, can make. I created these "Yi-isms" with the intentions of providing you with the necessary tools to enhance your desire for positive change in your life. Remember, positive change only comes about when we apply our free will to the desire for it.

I believe that when we acknowledge and focus on specific areas within our lives, only then do we possess the ability to achieve positive and necessary change.

This book should be used as a personal journal to help you achieve the change you wish to make. You will be given ample space to write your thoughts in this journal for the purpose of keeping yourself in balance. As you move forward with each "Yi-ism", it is important to take time to reflect upon your progress. This is an essential process which will allow you to acknowledge and value your own growth. This reflection is what I refer to as "Notes to Self." By utilizing these "Yi-isms" in this manner, self-growth and awareness are possible.

I hope you enjoy this process as much as I did when I created them.

San Dan Yi

Foreword

This book was created to help serve those who desire positive change and growth in their lives.

In these pages you will be provided with the necessary tools to see lasting positive change within you. This will happen by making choices in various areas of your life which will require that you review your own growth. As you begin your journey towards self-discovery, you will also experience the process of unfolding the layers which reveal your greater truths. These in turn, create greater clarity.

Once you are clear about your thinking and emotional processes, you will start to see the patterns of your behavior and viewpoints as well as of those who have had the most impact on you. Only then will you be able to walk through the doorway of new beginnings. You will be more confident now that you have the tools to accomplish exactly what you want from your life.

The bottom line is that this is about making good choices and your ability to "show up" in various areas of your life.

You will find that these succinct pearls of wisdom which I refer to as "Yi-isms", will help you to review your own patterns of behavior as well as those that are a part of your journey.

In addition, you will find that this journal for self-discovery will be one of your greatest companions along the path to personal-development. This will help you to transform your life positively. This process allows your inner life to mold your outer world experiences.

This collection of "Yi-isms" was created over several years from coaching thousands of clients all over the world. As I successfully helped these people, I was able to recognize the patterns and issues which kept them from having the life they would say they wanted.

I consider this journal to be a guide that can be used throughout your life. It will help you get on the right path and achieve positive results. So, let the journey begin!

With love,

San Dan Yi

San Dan Yi

∞

SECTION 1 PERSONAL GROWTH

Personal growth is the doorway where one begins the process of self-discovery and how we engage with others in our life. This is something that we need to learn to reflect upon. It is important to recognize that this is a journey and if we are to have the life that we say we want, we must make a concerted effort to incorporate activity that is conducive to achieve the desired results.

I hope you are excited about doing the work because it will lead you to greater personal growth and emotional freedom.

As we acknowledge and embrace our path towards personal growth, our horizons expand. Ego plays a key role for deciding how smoothly the journey will actually be. Although each person is special, every living thing has great value and serves a purpose. When we are in judgment of others, whether they have different belief systems or values than ours, isolation begins. Our path becomes more painful due to the ego's inability to cooperate which challenges our ability to co-exist.

Please use the following pages to list key people in your life. Write down whether or not you are making choices to judge, to not recognize, or honoring their beliefs systems. Pay attention to the issues and whether or not race, religion, sexuality, etc., is a factor. At some point, you may notice the very issues that annoy you about that person are a reflection of the very things that need improvement within yourself.

As you move forward, remember that it is ok to feel special. However, this does not mean that you are better than anyone else. Your journey is personal. Each person is also on a journey. It is important to remember that we are all a work in progress.

As we make progress, with each step of our journey, we develop confidence in who we are and view the people close to us (friends, family, etc.) more clearly. A key lesson from this process is to recognize that in order to love ourselves, we need to acknowledge drama, chaotic and self-defeating patterns of behavior for what they are. Negative patterns of behavior are nothing more than an individual's current inability to improve him or herself.

You may find that one of the biggest gifts that you can offer to someone you care about is the opportunity for self-improvement. It should be noted that the person must be ready to take the first step on that journey. It should not be forced because only when an individual is ready to make change can change happen.

Once that desire for change has been recognized, perhaps you can share your experiences to help inspire them to begin their own journal. Giving someone you care about the gift of inspiration is a way to show that you care without enabling any issues he or she may have.

In this section, consider the various scenarios in your life. If you find they are not positive or drain your energy, you have to make the decision as to what your "Movie" is and what it is not. Healthy love does not tear one down. It builds one up. It is important for personal growth on every level to acknowledge that life is like a movie and you are the director of that movie. You are responsible for all of the scenarios, for making all of the edits and producing the final cut.

Take some time to list some of the "Movies" that people are running in your life, ie: guilt, victimization, no value, poor me, etc. These "Movies" consist of negative emotions and self-deprecating words that bring you down. These are things that keep you from living up to your fullest potential. This is not to say that you should detach yourself from these people but rather, detach yourself from their own "Movie." This will allow you to view what they are presenting without bias. This will not only help you to see their dysfunction but help you to stop co-creating it with them.

You should always ask yourself the following question. Are others directing your "Movie" or are you the director of the "Movie?"

One suggestion to begin this process is to write down all of the people in your life and then write down what needs to change for the relationship to be healthy for you. There is no wrong way to use these pages because this is about your own personal journey.

If you are stooping, your support systems are not supplying you with the necessary confidence in yourself. This causes you to "Stoop, Not Stand." As we progress on our journey to self-awareness, we must look at ourselves and what we think may be holding us back from the life we desire.

Some of the questions you should ask yourself are:

- What are my support systems?
- Who are the key people that are part of that system?
- How stable and reliable are these support systems?
- Who is supplying the necessary tools for your personal growth?
- What do I feel I am lacking in my support systems?

Remember, it is important to have people in your life that will help you "Stand" tall with confidence. You do not want to people in your life that will beat you down, causing you to "Stoop" over when walking down your journey's path.

One of the most important processes in this journal is for you to recognize and embrace patterns of behavior which are not serving you. The best way an individual can see if the work he or she is doing is whether or not the work is having a positive effect on his or her life. This is the ability to look within yourself, without judging yourself. In other words, *"Look In, Not Out."*

To begin, define the areas you would like to change. The more one "Looks In" the less one "Looks Outward" and is fully accountable for their decision making processes. Most people who are not able to develop this ability fall into negative patterns of behavior which include self-loathing and the tendency to blame others for their misfortunes.

As you look inward and reflect upon various areas of your life, write a list of things you would like to change. One question you can ask yourself which will further guide you is whether or not the existing patterns of behavior are working for you, giving you the life you say you want. When you look inward, you should think about patterns of behavior such as: a smoker who wants good health, an overweight person who doesn't eat healthy foods, a person with financial issues who has poor money management skills, etc.

When you are looking outward you blame others for your problems. This is nothing more than an avoidance of "Looking In."

Some examples of this would be:

- I am overweight because my mother was a lousy cook and didn't teach me about proper nutrition.
- No matter how many times he tells me he is going to leave his wife, he still hasn't.
- Although I am struggling financially, gambling is an opportunity for me to improve my financial status.
- I don't get paid a fair wage because my boss doesn't see my value.
- My boy/girlfriend tells me s/he loves me but cheats on me.
- I don't see my family because I don't get along with some of them.
- Even though being neat makes me feel good about myself, I have too many other problems to worry about other than how clean my house is.

For many people, such myself, these three components for personal growth can be quite challenging. As we move forward while cleaning up "the runway of our life," we can view situations differently. This is a hallmark in our lives for several reasons. It is almost as though we are given a brand new set of eyes to see more clearly. We now have a new set of ears to listen with more distinction. These newly acquired skills allow us to create more positive and healthy choices for what we say we want for our lives.

Often people will take a vow of silence due to religious or other spiritual beliefs. When we are able to be still and remain silent, then we are able to better understand the subtle energies of our inner world and how it effects our outer world.

Take some "notes to self" regarding how your life is changing for the better, simply by applying the "Look, Listen and Learn" principles. This was one of my most favorite parts of my own journey towards self-growth. I believe it greatly improved my ability to help others as both a mentor and healer.

Some examples of this would be:

- I notice that my close friend's words and actions do not meet.
- My girl/boyfriend tells me that s/he only wants the best for me but continues to ignore my needs.
- My review at work was very good, however, I was passed over for a promotion by someone with fewer qualifications.
- I come from a close-knit family but when I need advice they can only give it to me from their perspective which is not in line with who I think I am but more in line with what they think I should be.

∞

SECTION 2 ABUNDANCE CONSCIOUSNESS

"If you don't look at yourself, you won't change."~San DanYi

Throughout my practice, I have observed some key differences between people who struggle financially and people who draw success into their life, almost seamlessly. At first I thought this was due to the old dogma viewpoints surrounding success such as if you get a good education, you will be able to hold onto your job. However, these are merely programmed psychological prisons that either we created or others created for us. It is a means for control.

Most of my clients that are well-off did not even have college educations! What they did have is an undying belief that they were on their path and living their passion. This made them so grateful or filled with gratitude and my struggling clients were filled with lamentations. Passion and belief are two key elements for building success. This results in a positive outlook as opposed to negative mental and emotional thought patterns.

Some examples of negative patterns are when you believe the following:

- I blame others for my misfortunes.
- I feel that I have no luck at all.
- I think that everyone is against me
- No matter how hard I try, I feel as though my efforts are never good enough.

Some examples of positive patterns are when you believe the following:

- I feel very fortunate because I love what I do.
- I am willing to make the time, energy and effort in order to make my goals become a reality.
- I feel that everyone around me is cooperating and supporting me.
- Money flows freely to me because my attitude towards it is positive.

Gratitude permits us to appreciate all the things we have. This process helps us to become a magnet that attracts:

- wealth,
- abundance,
- allows us to have happy, loving relationships,
- allows our children to grow up with positive attitudes,
- and allows us to live a life filled with vision and purpose.

Some examples would be:

- I am grateful for the love of my family and friends.
- I am grateful for my good health.
- I am grateful for the gift of life.
- I am grateful for having a full tank of gas in my car.
- I am grateful for the ability to buy healthy foods that I love to eat.
- I am grateful for a supporting and loving family.

Now that you have worked on your positive image only you can decide what is going to "Stand" in your way. Are you going to board the plane or are you going to wait in the "Stand By" line? In the end, you will find that the only obstacles that exist are all self-created. Look at your life as though you are at the airport (of your existence) and everyone around you has a ticket to board (the flight of their lives). Meanwhile, you stand still because you choose not to move forward because you are stuck. This is the same as waiting for a flight and being on "Standby."

If you are running a "Stand By" pattern, these are a few examples to consider.

- I am not good enough.
- I am not smart enough and motivated enough to be successful.
- I feel misunderstood by people around me.
- Happiness is not in the cards for me.
- I was married once and the marriage was a disaster. I am meant to be alone.
- Nobody gets it but me.
- I don't know why this always happens to me.

If the above describes your current situation and you wish to make the necessary changes, consider the following:

- I am deserving.
- I possess all of the skill sets necessary for the success I say I want.
- I bring a lot to the table in my relationship and I deserve emotional happiness.
- I am a good person.
- I create my own reality and no one else can do that but me.
- No one's going to stop me now.

Two key elements for achieving success in many areas of our lives are positive image and positive self-esteem. Without having a good self-image and a positive belief in ourselves, we will only shrink to the pressures of everyday life.

Some examples when you <u>don't</u> have positive self-imagery and esteem would be:

- No one in my family has ever amounted to anything. Why should I?
- I will never become a manager because I am not smart enough.
- Why am I always a bridesmaid and never a bride?
- For me, luck is a four letter word!
- If only I were thinner, I would find someone to love me.

Some examples when you <u>do</u> have a positive self-imager and self-esteem would be:

- I am in control of my own destiny.
- I feel I am the best candidate for the new position at work.
- I deserve a newer car.
- I deserve to live in a larger house.
- I create good fortune because I recognize opportunities when they present themselves.
- I know I will find someone who will love me just as I am.

Live to Give~

The consistent action of taking depletes the energy of replenishment. This is seen everywhere from the abuse of our environment, greed about money to special interest groups in politics. Empty wells do not feed life or create lasting bonds between all living things.

I know billionaires that barely have a dime to their name. They are billionaires in their consciousness and in their deeds. We can set the standards. We can become billionaires of the human condition.

This process is what makes the well run dry. It is because we constantly take and neglect to give. This is referred to as mutual receptivity. When you give and take, there is replenishment instead of exhaustion.

Some examples of "Live to Give" are:

- I am grateful that all of my needs are met. I want to give something back to my community.
- Even though I do not have a lot of money, I try to help people less fortunate.
- I may not have a lot of time but I do charitable work as often as I can.
- I value contributions no matter how big or small.
- I believe in the power of paying it forward.
- Good deeds come back to me in positive ways.

∞

SECTION 3 HEALTHY RELATIONSHIPS

This section has been created for those who wish to recognize the negative patterns of behavior that prevent them from being in the relationship they say they want.

By reflecting upon these "Yi-isms," you will be able recognize behavior that needs to change in order for you to have healthy relationships. This applies to all kinds of relationships, whether it is with a family member or friend.

If you are not sure whether or not your relationship is healthy, ask yourself the following questions:

- My relationship with my significant other does not match what I say I want for myself.
- Do you find yourself making excuses for your partner?
- Do you accept things as they are even though you know the situation does not serve you?
- Do you find yourself making excuses such as it is what it is?
- Can I communicate more positively with the people that I care about?
- Is it necessary for me to yell to be heard?
- Do I need to repeat myself in order for someone to understand me?
- Am I reacting to others or are they reacting to me?
- Am I responding to others or are they responding to me?
- Do people easily push my buttons?
- Do I get the silent treatment when I am not in agreement with my loved ones?

Date Up Not Down

The term "Date Up Not Down" refers to our perception of a relationship and its potential to be a long term one. "Date Up" refers to the positive things sought from a potential partner when dating. These attributes include good communication, affection, emotional availability, trustworthiness, honesty, integrity, compassion, consideration, great intimacy, etc.. It basically refers to the things we say we want.

When angst ensues frequently in a relationship this is what is meant by "Dating Down."This is typically found when dating someone who is emotionally unavailable, does not communicate, bickers, is not affectionate, is not reliable, trustworthy, honest, considerate, faithful, etc.

Have you ever been in a relationship where you feel that you are settling? You would be amazed how many people do settle. Usually at the core of this are aspects of low self-esteem and low self-worthiness. The more work you do on yourself, the more you are able to see clearly. This, in turn, will supply you with the necessary tools in order to make the changes needed for a healthy relationship. When we learn to "Date Up", we ask for more from our partners because we are capable of giving more.

Take some time to think about how you have changed. Make a list of how you have settled in the past. Include as much detail as you can remember. Then make a list of ways in which you have grown. Remember, you cannot change something unless you can identify the changes that need to be made.

At this point in the journal, proving that you have made the choice to complete all of the exercises, you should have a clearer outlook regarding your relationships. You should be able to determine whether or not your relationships are healthy, create happiness in your life or need to change. As we explore the next group of "Yi-isms," you will be provided with the tools to better understand how to achieve your goals towards having the relationship you say you want.

As we get healthier and more balanced, we are able to identify the areas which are out of balance, one-sided or not serving us. We can also learn to express these needs to our partner from a place of responding and reacting as opposed to what is missing in the relationship. Remember, you cannot be responsible for another's journey of self-discovery. However, only you can be accountable and responsible for yours.

As yourself the following:

- When we go out, am I always paying the bill?
- I am affectionate but I have to prompt my partner to show me affection.
- I always initiate every activity between us.
- The only time my loved one calls is when he or she needs something.
- I make a lot of effort to communicate clearly only to find that the person I am trying to reach barely responds and it negatively impacts our relationship.

Some positive examples of "Mutual Receptivity" are:

- My relationships are based upon a good balance between give and take.
- Even though my partner and I have our differences, we balance each other in many ways.
- We encourage each other as often as we need it.
- I feel that my partner has my back covered and I have his/hers.
- We both have similar goals and support each other's endeavors.
- I found the perfect team player in my mate.

Usually you will notice in many relationships around you that they become mirrors from early childhood on that mold and shape our viewpoints of how relationships should be. Many people who are in abusive relationships are in them because they are trying to work on things within themselves but are taught at an early age that staying in abusive relationships are healthy and based on love. This could not be further from the truth! You have bought into programming and unhealthy programming at that.

Abuse comes in many forms whether physical, mental and or emotional. One can never find happiness and joy from this path. The best way to see if you have or are currently in an abusive relationship have written dialogue with yourself and identify the abusive aspects of your past relationships with family friends and lovers then bring it forward into the current moments to see if those patterns and trends are still continuing.

If there is one single negative pattern of behavior that destroys any kind of relationship, it is the inability to recognize the needs of others. The reason that one person reacts to another is because there are unrecognized issues present. The reaction is caused due to the need to control the other person. At best, this is a sophisticated form of bullying. This can cause a person to shut down and withdraw.

The following negative examples which demonstrate this behavior are:

- When I am expressing myself, my partner cuts me off and doesn't allow me to finish my thought.
- If I ask a simple question, my partner raises his/her voice so s/he doesn't have to answer it.
- When I state my opinion about anything, my partner responds by telling me that I don't know what I am talking about.
- If I challenge something my partner says, s/he will tell me that I am wrong.
- If my partner is upset with me, my mother will tell me that I must have done something wrong to deserve it.

Responding in a positive caring manner permits for better communication in our relationships. Better communication leads to a more solid relationship based upon admiration, mutual respect and trust.

The following are positive examples of "*Respond; Don't React.*"

- My partner is yelling at me because s/he does not agree with my viewpoints. I am letting him/her know in a nice manner that it is not necessary to yell in order because I am not going to stop expressing my opinions.
- When my partner tells me that I do not know what I am talking about, I respond by saying that s/he is the only one that sees me in this light. I am not in agreement with his/her viewpoint of me.
- When my partner wants to stay home and watch television all evening, I don't criticize him/her for it. I simply go ahead and do the things I enjoy doing.
- When my partner tries to push my buttons, I simply inform him/her that I am choosing not to participate in the drama.

∞

SECTION 4 RESPONSIBILITY TO YOURSELF

This is an essential part of your journey towards self-growth and self-improvement. It is necessary for the following "Yi-isms" to be completed at this point in order for the process to come full circle.

At this point, provided that you have already completed the previous sections of this journal, you should be willing and ready to acknowledge that you are fully responsible and accountable for the life you say you want.

Remember, everywhere you look in the outer world today, nations, leaders of nations and the people of nations are all being asked to be accountable and to have responsibility unto themselves. Without this process, people never truly understand how we are all truly connected.

This is my favorite part of the journal! On the following pages, review the progress you have made and make a list of any area you feel you need to work on. Be honest with yourself. It is ok to review old issues and acknowledge that you now know how to handle those issues differently. This is part of the growth process.

It is important to acknowledge the need to fully show up in your life for the simple reason that it is your life! If you can't show up in your own life, who will?

Ask yourself the following questions:

- Am I willing to make every effort to change, no matter what?
- Do I have the ability to think about my actions, words and deeds and how they serve me on my journey without bias?
- Can I work with others in a cooperative manner?
- Can I fully show up to make the necessary changes happen?
- If I don't take care of my health, who will?
- I am learning to be more independent and less co-dependent.

Movement happens when we make choices and display a willingness for change. There are many areas in our life which need constant movement in order to "chart and plot a course" towards a fulfilling life. This "Yi-ism" is designed to help you acknowledge the importance of health. Without a strong mind and a healthy body, all goals equate to nothing more than a mere illusion. The more we keep things moving and flowing, the quicker all of our goals can become a reality.

Ask yourself the following questions:

- Am I making healthy choices all the time about the food that I eat?
- Do I have more good habits for health than bad?
- Do I eat too much?
- Do I drink too much?
- Am I physically incapacitated because of my poor health choices?
- Am I a victim of my poor health choices or are the choices fully my responsibility?

If we do not develop the ability to track and review our growth processes, we put our overall ability to grow and achieve our goals in jeopardy. The key to this achievement is the ability to "Show Up" in every area of our lives. Without this ability, we may fall into self-defeating, negative patterns of behavior and viewpoints that we are trying to eliminate.

Some examples of NOT "Showing Up" are:

- I didn't get the brakes fixed on my car and now my mechanic has informed me that the damage to the car is greater, costing me more money.
- I waited too long to book the tickets for the cruise and now the cabin I wanted is no longer available.
- My children will not be able to attend summer camp because I neglected to enroll them on time.
- I was fired from my job because I couldn't finish the projects in time, even though I was given ample time.
- I waited 'til the last minute to do my term paper and received a lower grade than I am capable of.
- I didn't pay my auto insurance on time and my policy was canceled.
- I was in a rush to a meeting and forgot to fill up my tank only to wind up getting stuck on the side of the road which made me lose the account.

Some examples of "Showing Up" are:

- I pay my bills on the first of the month and am in good standing with all of the companies that I do business with.
- When I have a project, I begin to work on it immediately and schedule time to work on it so that I will be able to submit it on time.
- I plan things in advance and always allow time in case of unforeseen circumstances.
- When it comes to my children's needs, I always make them a priority.
- My annual health check-ups are planned well in advance.
- I constantly educate myself about the latest health innovations because my health and my family's health is a priority.

Surrender To Yourself~

Surrendering is a process in which we let go of things that no longer serve us. It is about our own needs, not the other person's. It is an act of loving yourself. Sometimes, when we get out of the way and don't push so hard, things happen more quickly for us. We become more patient with our shortcomings and our accomplishments.

"Surrender to yourself" means to be kind to ourselves on our journey without any complacency. Surrender also permits goals and achievements to happen almost as if it were magical.

By using this journal, you are willing to look at areas of your life that need to changed. This should be done with kindness and compassion for yourself and towards the people who are currently unable to recognize the things they need to.

Surrender will take you out of:

- frustration,
- self-loathing ,
- will open up new doorways inside of yourself on the journey of self-discover and self-love,
- judgment towards yourself and others,
- feeling less disappointment in your life by your processes.

On the following pages, list the areas in your life where you can surrender and allow the necessary processes of movement to take place. Also, in this section, you should list the areas of your life where you have surrendered and what the results were.

About San DanYi

San DanYi's conscious spiritual awakening started when he was introduced to the teachings of Torkum Saraydarian. In 1985, he attended Torkum's Sedona, Arizona ashram named, "The Aquarian Educational Group." It was here that San DanYi first discovered a greater meaning to his life. Through Torkum's literary body of work, he realized the purpose of life was to strive for contact with the soul's guidance and destiny. Through meditation, moment-to-moment conscious awareness and the practice of taking vows of silence, San DanYi came to realize that the ultimate journey for humankind is to achieve self-realization. Part of this realization is the need to serve and help one another through kindness, compassion, and love.

San DanYi is a great believer in the working legacy of the late Paramahansa Yogananda. After reading Yogananda's "Divine Romance," San DanYi found a greater joy and bliss through the deeper understanding and connection with source. No longer seeking outer world fulfillment, San DanYi realized his life's purpose is to show people how their desirous and ego-based realities keep them prisoners in a smaller existence, which resides in a larger, and sometimes undiscovered universe.

Today, San DanYi travels worldwide, offering individual and group counseling and private retreats. He speaks on such topics as: abundance consciousness, life path fulfillment and teaches meditation and visualization techniques, which promote a more dynamic life experience.

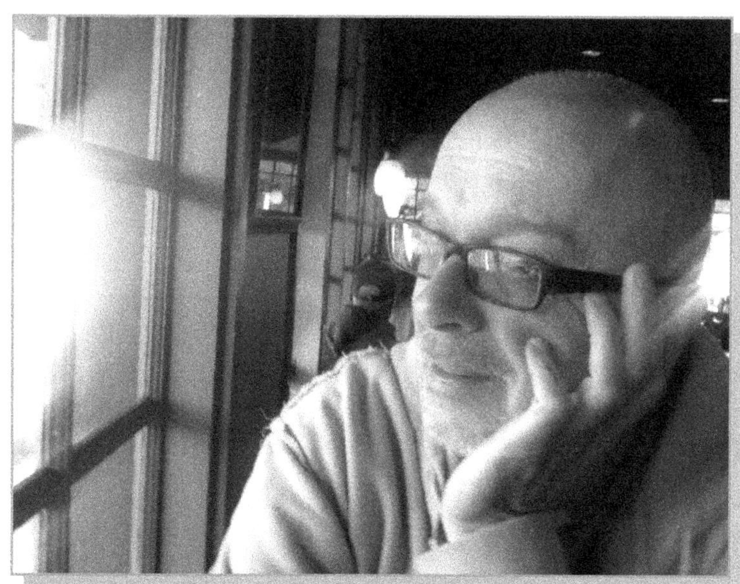

www.ingramcontent.com/pod-product-compliance
Lightning Source LLC
Chambersburg PA
CBHW062041090426
42740CB00016B/2981

9780615964577